Library of
Davidson College

AN AMBIVALENT HERITAGE
Euro-American Relations

Peter Duignan and L. H. Gann

HOOVER INSTITUTION
on War, Revolution and Peace

Stanford University
1994

The Hoover Institution on War, Revolution and Peace, founded at Stanford University in 1919 by President Herbert Hoover, is an interdisciplinary research center for advanced study on domestic and international affairs in the twentieth century. The views expressed in its publications are entirely those of the authors and do not necessarily reflect the views of the staff, officers, or Board of Overseers of the Hoover Institution.

Hoover Essay No. 7

Copyright © 1994 by the Board of Trustees of the
 Leland Stanford Junior University
Material contained in this essay may be quoted with appropriate citation.

First printing, 1994

Manufactured in the United States of America

98 97 96 95 94   9 8 7 6 5 4 3 2 1

Library of Congress Cataloging-in-Publication Data

Duignan, Peter.
 An ambivalent heritage : Euro-American relations / Peter Duignan and L. H. Gann
   p.   cm. — (Hoover essays ; no. 7)
 Includes bibliographical references.
 ISBN 0-8179-3702-1
 1. Europe—Relations—United States. 2. United States—Civilization—European influences. 3. United States—Relations—Europe. 4. Europe—Civilization—American influences. I. Gann, Lewis H., 1924– .
   II. Title. III. Series: Hoover essays (Stanford, Calif. : 1992) ; no. 7.
D1065.U5D84   1994   94–5916
303.48'27304—dc20   CIP

Executive Summary

From its beginning, the relationship between Europe and America has been marked by profound ambivalence. Europe (especially Britain) was both admired and resented, held up for imitation and cursed. For much of American history Europe was respected for its culture, aristocratic manners, eloquence, and social prestige but feared for its class struggles, authoritarianism, state religions, and fratricidal wars. The Europeans felt Americans were uncouth, excessively individualistic, and violent. Although the upper classes were often anti-American, the working class initially viewed the United States as the land of opportunity, equality, and freedom.

The United States became the world's most successful multiracial and multiethnic society, but its roots were European (over 80 percent of Americans derive from European stock). The culture, laws, and institutitutions also largely came from Europe, especially from Britain. But although Europe greatly influenced the United States until World War II, thereafter the United States has shaped Europe. And although for much of American history, Europe was a mecca for American artists and literati, after World War II American culture became more self-confident and assertive—a reflection of U.S. military and economic might. No longer would the United States shy away from involvement with Europe; instead the United States determined to stay in Europe, rebuild it, and pressure the Europeans into economic cooperation through a customs union and into the military alliance through the North Atlantic Treaty Organization (NATO). NATO would protect Europeans from the Soviet Union and from one another. The result is a partial Americanization of Europe and the dominance of American culture, technology, business methods, and science. American power and influence created a good deal of hostility, especially from the British and French, who resented the loss of their leadership. But overall, American and Europeans respected each other, depended on each other, and created, by massive reciprocal relationships, the Atlantic Community, the greatest political economic and cultural association in world history.

AN AMBIVALENT HERITAGE
Euro-American Relations

Introduction

Most Americans have always regarded Europe as the continent from which they traced their ancestry. As American historian Daniel J. Boorstin put it, "our roots were European; we got our religion, common law, constitutionalism and political ideals of liberty, justice and equality from Europe." Americans equally derived their fears of aristocrats, feudalism, and monopoly from Europe. The vast size and wealth of the American continent and its pioneering history tended to make Americans more confident, self-reliant, and individualistic than Europeans. European travelers to America traditionally stressed Americans' untoward bumptiousness. But at the same time, Americans felt insecure and culturally inferior compared with Europeans. Despite Americans' reputation for national exuberance they have periodically experienced moods of national despondency that were more profound in the nineteenth than in the twentieth century. As a diarist put it just before the outbreak of the Civil War, "We are a weak, divided, disgraced people, unable to maintain our national existence. . . .It's a pity we ever renounced our allegiance to the British Crown."[1] Despite periodic recurrences of national melancholy, the achievements of World War II brought about a major change in attitude: Americans became more confident in their experiment. They wanted to export the advantages of their system to the world at large and increasingly believed, at least until the Vietnam War, in the worth, even the superiority, of U.S. culture, political and economic systems, science, and technology.[2]

The United States began as an outgrowth of Europe—more specifically, a British colony. The first English people to settle permanently on this side of the Atlantic arrived at Jamestown in 1607. British sovereignty thereafter extended over what later became the thirteen colonies—a loose chain of territories wedged between the Atlantic Ocean and the Allegheny Mountains. British America would stay under the British Crown for more than a century and a half, a time as long as that which elapsed between the enunciation of the Monroe Doctrine in 1823 and the present day. A lexicographer such as Noah Webster might stress the peculiarity of the American language (in his *American Dictionary*, 1828); but in fact American English never diverged from British English in the same way Afrikaans diverges from High Dutch. Britain, its empire, and the United States remained linked by a common tongue and culture that would become strongly influenced by American usage.

The mutual impact was profound. Americans accepted from Britain not only folkways, language, and culture but also a legal system based on British Common Law, British parliamentary institutions, and British local government. The founding fathers had all been born British subjects; they discussed politics according to the norms familiar to educated English of a liberal disposition. Well-schooled Americans of the period had read Shakespeare and Milton; they were familiar with the King James Bible and the *Book of Common Prayer*, which deeply influenced American as well as British thought and speech. American lawyers had read great British jurists such as Sir William Blackstone. Literate Americans were familiar with the philosophy of Locke and Hume. Americans and British people read the same folktales and the same nursery rhymes, sang the same tunes, and had the same traditions of voluntarism and religious diversity. When Americans took up arms against the British Crown, they fought in defense of what they considered the liberties due to true English citizens, liberties previously secured by the English Parliament against the English king during the seventeenth century.

Although Anglo-America would come to dominate most of

North America, observers living in 1750 would have found such a forecast surprising. Two hundred and fifty years ago, a prophet might well have predicted that the heirs of Spain, dominant in most of South America, Central America, and what is now the American Southwest, would win the struggle for continental supremacy. Others might have bet on the French, who occupied a huge belt of territory stretching from Canada along the Mississippi Valley down to New Orleans and the Gulf of Mexico. But it was the English-speaking peoples who won out in the course of extended conflicts; English traditions of constitutional government prevailed over royal absolutism or the trust in centralized government that characterized France and Spain.

But though the bulk of North America remained English speaking, great differences arose between America and the homeland. Britain was a monarchy supported by a hereditary aristocracy and an established church. The American colonists rejected all these institutions. Within the United Kingdom, as constituted at the time of the War of Independence, there were few immigrants and slavery was outlawed. The United States, by contrast, had substantial foreign minorities (especially Germans) and a small African-American population, mostly enslaved. From the beginnings of American settler society, American relations with Britain, and indeed with Europe as a whole, were marked by profound ambivalence.

The American War of Independence was indeed the first American civil war. In the thirteen colonies, all those who would not or could not fit into the American political culture and middle-class society—many of the rich and well born at the top, as well as outsiders such as Native Americans, Scottish Highlanders, poverty-stricken tenant farmers, and some African Americans—sided with the king against those colonists who backed the Continental Congress and General Washington. European opinion was likewise split. All those who accounted themselves as progressives, as *philosophes*, or as moderate reformers were apt to see the future with the United States. By contrast, it was "church and king" mobs that burned the houses of pro-American sympathizers in England.

George Washington's farewell address (1796) warned against "passionate attachments" to specific countries; it did not set the United States on an isolationist course, however. It was Thomas

Jefferson in his first inaugural address (1801) who emphasized no "entangling alliances" with foreign governments. The War of 1812 with Britain reinforced American distrust and determination to resist foreign interference in the Western Hemisphere—hence the Monroe Doctrine (1823). One reason the United States refused to take part in the anti–slave trade campaign after 1807 was bitter memories of British seizure and search tactics. In fact, it was the British claim to the right to search suspected slave ships that was a major cause of the War of 1812. Not until the Webster-Ashburton Treaty of 1842 was the issue solved: an African American squadron was delegated to stop American ships suspected of carrying slaves. Thus America again began cooperating with European powers, and the isolationist spirit in the United States weakened. Throughout the history of the United States, national interests have impelled American presidents and Congress to actively engage with foreign states. American foreign policy has always aimed to keep the nation whole and indivisible, to protect its borders and frontiers, to keep hostile foreign powers out of North America, and to ensure American commerce access to markets and resources worldwide.[3]

From its beginning a free-trading America sought to buy and sell throughout the world. Commodore Matthew C. Perry opened up Japan to American commerce after 1854, and at the Berlin Conference of 1884–1885, the United States insisted that the Congo region be a free-trade area. Then, in 1899, Secretary of State John Hay proclaimed an open door policy for trade with China. In World Wars I and II the Americans returned to Europe to fight alongside the democracies. After World War II, the United States fought for global trade liberalization through the General Agreement on Tariffs and Trade (GATT). The United States, then, has never been a truly isolationist nation but rather a neutralist one.

European Views of America

From the late nineteenth century on, however, despite numerous diplomatic disputes between Britain and the United States, a special relationship developed between the two countries, much closer than, say, the relationship between Spain and the Argentine or

France and Quebec. Upper-class Americans took the British upper class as their model: Harvard and Yale prided themselves on their affinity to Oxford and Cambridge. Americans have always drawn heavily on British books; many a rich American in the late nineteenth century boasted of marrying his daughter to a British aristocrat with a splendid title and an empty purse. The U.S.-Canadian frontier remained unfortified, setting up an intimate connection between U.S. and Canadian expansion to the West as settlers crossed and recrossed the frontier without hindrance.

In return, many Europeans admired, even idealized America. Goethe, a German poet, apostrophized the United States at the beginning of the last century in a poem entitled *Amerika, du hast es besser*: "America, you are better off than we are; may God preserve you in future from Europe's mournful legacy, from romantic ruins, from tales of bandits, knights, and ghosts." America, Alexis de Tocqueville had written admiringly (1834–40), may justly boast of "a marvellous combination . . . the spirit of religion and the spirit of freedom." Religion supplies to freedom "the divine source of its right." Freedom also stands indebted to those many newcomers "who came in waves to plant themselves on the shores of the New World. . . . When the immigrants left their motherland, they had no idea of any superiority of some over others. It is not the happy or the powerful who go into exile, and poverty with misfortune is the best-known guarantee of equality among men."[4]

Tocqueville may have somewhat romanticized America, but he was rarely wrong. Religion affected American political culture in many ways. Pastors and church elders left their imprint, both in promoting moral idealism and in giving American politics and academe a peculiar touch of self-righteousness. Equally important, as Tocqueville had stressed, was the role of the immigrants. These men and women had come to the United States for economic, political, religious, or racial reasons; they had crossed the ocean to escape the authority of nobles, monarchs, religious authorities, landlords, and, more recently, commissars. (Anticommunism in America was strengthened by successive waves of refugees from Eastern Europe, China, Cuba, and Vietnam.) Generally speaking, these newcomers were ambivalent toward their respective countries of origin but were self-consciously patriotic toward the land of their adoption. Americans—on the whole—were accustomed to self-help and more respectful toward the self-made man or woman than most Europeans. Americans were for self-improvement, were informed, and were active in self-government and voluntarism. J. S. Mill and Tocqueville said that Americans were self-reliant, individualistic, practical people; they were also joiners and pluralists from many different cultures. Americans were also used to striking differences of wealth and familiar with ethnic and religious prejudice. But the country was too vast and varied to permit the emergence of a nationally recognized upper class. An old family in Boston counted for nothing in Los Angeles. High ranks in the civil service and the armed forces did not carry the same prestige as they did in Europe. The average Texan or Nevadan might not even recognize the names of eastern prestige schools such as Phillips Exeter Academy in New Hampshire or Hotchkiss School in Connecticut.

That system made for a surprising degree of stability given the enormous disparities that divided U.S. society. Until recently, Americans voted more often—in national, state, and local elections—than the citizens of any other country. There was a great army of unpaid activists. (During the 1960 presidential elections, for instance, some 4,000,000 volunteers were busy organizing rallies, ringing doorbells, mailing envelopes, and so on.) Each presidential, each gubernatorial candidate had to create or rebuild a personal organization in a country where people moved often over enormous distances. The American system accommodated flux in a way that no European system could rival. It gave temporary places of prominence to an extraordinarily large number of people and provided for political alliances of the strangest kind, even alliances that might cut across ideological divisions. Kipling, the bard of the empire, puzzled over the American spirit's strange shifts of mood

> That bids him flout the Law he makes,
> That bids him make the Law he flouts
> Till, dazed by many doubts, he wakes
> The drumming guns that have no doubts.[5]

But even Kipling had no doubts that the American spirit would find salvation at last.

Lord Bryce, in *The American Commonwealth* (1888), wanted the United States to be a world power and its democratic system to spread to Europe. Israel Zangwill, an Anglo-Jewish writer, at the end of the century called America God's crucible, the great melting pot that would fuse and reform the European peoples, an attitude reflected by the countless immigrants who flocked to the United States from Europe during the nineteenth and the twentieth centuries. The America of fact did not always turn out to be the *goldene medinah*, the golden state of the Jews, or the *Land der unbegrenzten Möglichkeiten*, the land of unlimited opportunities of the Germans. Nevertheless, they came by the millions—Germans, Scandinavians, Irish, and later, people from Eastern and Southern Europe including Poles, Russians, Jews, Italians, and Greeks. At the turn of the century, there was also a massive increase in the number of Spanish-speaking people (not so much Spaniards from Europe as Mexicans and, after World War II, Puerto Ricans and Cubans), as well as newcomers from the Far East.

The precise ethnic makeup of the American people is hard to disentangle because of intermarriage and murky ethnic and racial boundaries. By the time of the 1980 census, 50 million persons reported themselves to be of English origin (the largest single group), but more than half of those listed other ethnic origins as well. The same applied to the 49 million who put down German and to those who described themselves as Scottish or Welsh by descent. Three-quarters of the 40 million Americans who categorized themselves as Irish also reported other ancestries; the same went for 4 million Swedes and for a majority of the 3.5 million Norwegians. Twelve million said that they were of Italian origin, but only 7 million of those indicated exclusively Italian ancestry. A majority of the 8 million who claimed Polish ancestry also reported forebears of other nationalities:[6] But despite massive recent immigration from Latin America and Asia, something like four-fifths of the U.S. population remains of European origin (including that large proportion of Hispanics who describe themselves as "white" on the census forms). These boundaries remain tenuous. No matter what their nationality, Americans would marry whom they pleased (but usually before World War II within the same religious cohort).

Despite their diverse ethnic roots, the great majority of

Americans stayed in the land of their adoption. They took up citizenship and came to feel at home in a country whose people were not expected to know their place but would rather make their place. Immigration created ethnic lobbies of a specifically American kind. Naturalized citizens used their political influence to help the cause of their kinfolk in Europe: Irish Americans supported the cause of Irish independence against Britain; Polish Americans agitated against the rule of the Russian czars, Jews strove for Israel; and Czechs moved against the Hapsburgs. Immigration also acted as a spur to further immigration, as newcomers commonly helped other relatives and friends to make the long journey across the Atlantic. Indeed, immigrants' letters to friends and relatives at home provided more accurate and relevant information about the United States than a great many academic tomes on the subject.

The United States thus always seemed a land of opportunity to foreigners and immigrants seeking the "American dream." The United States was the first great nation to achieve modernization in the sense of eliminating hereditary class distinctions, reducing class barriers, opening up equal opportunities, and creating a mass consumer society.

Of course, there were many critics. From the early beginnings of their country, Americans were derided as uncouth and lawless; later they were widely portrayed as nouveaux riches even more than those wealthy Argentinians and Creoles who were satirized in the light comedies of nineteenth-century France. Americans were supposedly materialistic, brash, Philistine. Their society was said to be artificial, without organic links, lacking both a traditional peasantry and an aristocracy rooted in the soil. Americans were eternally restless, always on the move. Americans were reportedly greedy, crude, devoid of tragic imagination. They had no respect for their betters. Neither Heinrich Heine, a romantic revolutionary, nor Jakob Burckhardt, an imaginative conservative, could stand America. "When good Americans die, they go to Paris," Oscar Wilde scoffed in *A Woman of No Importance*. "Indeed? And where do bad Americans go? Oh, they go to America!" Americans had other supposed failings. They were insufferable in their moral pretentiousness, a characteristic that they were thought to share with their English cousins. "Corruption, Immorality, Irreligion, and above all, Self Interest" ruled the United States, argued an aristocratic British diplomat at the beginning of the nineteenth century. "There is no faith and no knowledge of the Lord amongst most of our brethren; in the United States the younger generation inherit nothing from their parents except what is needed to make their way in this world," echoed an Orthodox Jewish visitor from Eastern Europe at the end of the century.[7]

In theory, the British should have been the most pro-American among Europeans—Britons and Americans were so-called cousins. As we pointed out earlier, many Americans were indeed Anglophiles, especially upper-class people from the East Coast. But their sentiments were not necessarily reciprocated in Britain. Indeed, the traditional British establishment was apt to look down on Americans as brash and uncultured. (Some old-fashioned Tories, for example, criticized Winston Churchill on the grounds that he was half-American.) Qualities regarded as virtuous in the United States—enthusiasm, dedication to hard work, openness, and lack of class consciousness—seemed vices to a great many old-fashioned, upper-class British people, though not to the bulk of British workers.

Views hostile to the United States were widespread in Europe at large; indeed, there was a curious continuity in European critiques concerning America and the Americans. Long before the thirteen colonies attained their independence, Swiss immigrants found that *alles ist ganz anders hier* (everything is quite different here). Many liked the change—freedom from caste distinctions, higher living standards, personal freedom:

> In this country anyone who gains riches, gold and silver, is esteemed like a lord in Europe.... I shall never return to Switzerland as long as I live, for I have come to a goodly land.... Evidently I have done well by my children in having left my fatherland, and for this I thank God eternally. We live under a goodly and gentle government. Provisions are plentiful; there are no tithes and no labor services; speech is free.[8]

But there was another side to America. Woe betide those who did not make good, who missed their families in the old country, or who longed for security and accepted custom.

In this country there are innumerable religions—Reformed, Sabbatarians, Tumblers, Quakers, Atheists who have no religion, no churches and no schools, who believe neither in God nor the Devil, in Heaven or Hell. There are also countless tongues here English, Swedish, Gaelic, High German, Low German, Dutch... This is a refuge for exiled sectarians, an asylum for all manner of evil-doers from Europe, a confusing Babel, a refuge for unclean spirits, a homestead for Satan, in truth a new Sodom.

Likewise Charles Dilke, an English Radical who toured the United States during the 1860s. He described Americans in terms normally associated with postindustrial America. Americans were foolishly permissive toward their children, who "never dream of work out of school hours, or of solid reading that is not compulsory" and, as a rule, turn out to be "forward, ill mannered, and immoral."[9] American women were too independent; crime was rife in America; American courts combined excessive legalism with excessive leniency; there were too many foreign immigrants not likely to be absorbed in the general population. Americans were addicted to strange cults that appealed not just to the poor and the ignorant but to solid citizens who ought to know better. Americans were too soft to fight. (At the outbreak of the Mexican-American War in 1846, European military opinion thus widely predicted an American defeat, as did the London *Times*.) America offended, above all, the rich and the well-born. As Charles Francis Adams, the U.S. minister in London, explained during the U.S. Civil War, "the great body of the aristocracy and the commercial classes are anxious to see the United States go to pieces while the middle and lower classes sympathize with us."[10]

From the end of the nineteenth century, there were two new twists to anti-American sentiment. Americans intervened in countries where they were not wanted. "To whom do I owe the displeasure of this intrusion," Dame Europe coldly asks Uncle Sam (according to a British cartoon of the Cuban war of 1898). "My name is Uncle Sam," goes the reply. "Any relation of the late Colonel Monroe?" (President James Monroe, framer of the Monroe Doctrine), Dame Europe chillingly responds.[11] Above all, there were attacks from the left. According to Marx, who admired the United States, the American colonization of California (taken forcibly from Mexico), the occupation of Australia, and the opening of China and Japan were progressive developments, part of the historic task incumbent on the bourgeoisie to establish a world market and a global system of production.[12] Thereafter, self-styled progressive opinion in Europe underwent a decisive shift, as European socialists debated at length the contradictions of U.S. monopoly capitalism. They also wondered why an advanced capitalist country such as the United States failed to develop a great revolutionary movement or at least a solidly proletarian party among the disinherited mass of immigrants. Few of these critics accepted the commonsense explanation that the great majority of immigrants liked what they found and had no wish to make fundamental political changes. The real or assumed deficiencies of the American working class were explained in terms of a false consciousness imposed on them by their masters. The American—like the Jew—was equated with the city slicker, the huckster, the rootless cosmopolitan. By the end of the nineteenth century, the entire ideology and vocabulary of anti-Americanism was already well in place.

American Views of Europe

The Americans were as ambivalent about Europe as Europeans were about America. Americans were immigrants. Immigrants from whatever country are apt to look on their own or their ancestors' homeland with some degree of nostalgia. But immigrants also leave home for some good cause—whether poverty, persecution, or mere boredom. Thus, the old country may be remembered with dislike, at times with blank hatred. Europe at its best was respected for culture, aristocratic elegance, and social prestige. By the end of the last century, Britain and, to a lesser extent, France had become the mecca of American artists, literati, social climbers, and millionaires who married their sons to the daughters of aristocratic families. London was associated with the best of men's tailoring; Paris, with feminine elegance and avant-garde art; Berlin and Göttingen, with scholarship. (Later, in American movies, foreign accents were de rigueur for wicked countesses, pastry cooks, psychiatrists, and vampires.) On a more serious note, Americans owed a profound debt to European science, art, and scholarship, as well as industrial skills, business enterprise, and investment. Throughout the nineteenth century, the United States remained a massive importer of European, especially British, capital.

From their country's beginning, Americans had seen themselves as a new nation, with new laws and a new and free polity. The French observer Crèvecoeur had long ago insisted, in his *Letters from an American Farmer* (1782), that America had transformed Europeans into new people unburdened by respect for duchesses, counts, bishops, or churches. Yet a great many American intellectuals did not share his optimism. They felt they lived in a cultural wilderness that lacked Europe's great past. For culture and tradition, educated Americans had long looked to Europe, and thousands had crossed the Atlantic to find in Europe inspiration, training, or a more sophisticated way of life. Indeed, it was not until after World War II that American culture became self-confident and assertive—in part a reflection of U.S. military and economic power.

There was, however, another side to the coin. Europe was also regarded as a potential menace. Sophisticated and supercilious European diplomatists were suspected of wishing to involve innocent Americans in foreign wars not of their making. Popery, libertinism, and unbelief, in addition to subversion and revolt, were associated at various times with Europe by frightened nativists. The fear was that Europe might corrupt America, which was intended by God (claimed John Winthrop) as a "city built upon a hill, the eyes of all people are upon us." Above all, Americans, themselves descended from immigrants, have been ambivalent about each generation of new immigrants—usually poorer and less skilled than the old-timers.

> Wide open and unguarded stand our gates
> And through them presses a wild and motley throng—
> Men from the Volga and the Tartar steppes,
> Featureless figures from the Hoang-ho,
> Malayan, Scythian, Teuton, Celt, and Slav
> Fleeing the Old World's poverty and scorn.

That poem by Thomas Bailey Aldrich, written a century ago,

struck an answering chord among many of his countrypeople who dreaded the strange-looking newcomers from Europe and elsewhere. The immigrants were feared on many grounds—as competitors willing to depress the American workers' living standards by working for lower wages and also as potential subversives, "hyphenated Americans," with no loyalty to their country of adoption. In fact, these suspicions were misconceived. Militants among the immigrants formed a small minority. The great majority had no intention of overthrowing the republic that had given them refuge; they looked for advancement through individual effort, not to a revolutionary transformation of society. Nevertheless, stereotypes concerning subversion, libertinism, and unbelief were at various times associated with Europe by nativist opinion—as was popery, or Catholicism.

Throughout American history, ethnic preferences have shifted in time, with the most recent arrivals usually being the most unpopular. By the end of the last century, for example, Scandinavians had found acceptance; jokes about dumb Swedes were replaced by taunts at stupid Poles or Italians (who by then did much of the unskilled work previously associated with Northern European immigrants). Then came jeers at Jews who were moving into the textile and other light industries. The foreigners least distrusted by the end of the nineteenth century were the British. This would have surprised Americans who had lived through the Revolutionary War or the Anglo-American War of 1812, at which time patriotic propaganda described the British as brutal, supercilious, and hypocritical. (Indeed, many British immigrants, disliking their native country's class structure, were just as vocal in their criticism.) Anti-British sentiments were reinforceed during the late nineteenth century by Irish newcomers full of hatred for their homeland's British oppressors. There was also trouble during the U. S. Civil War when the British upper class (as distinct from the workers) was apt to side with the South, while John Bull was denounced in the United States as

> Ever victorious
> Haughty, vainglorius
> Snobbish, censorious,
> Great John Bull.[13]

But throughout the nineteenth century British immigrants—farmers, professional people, artisans, and skilled workers—kept coming to the United States. (Indeed, far more people migrated to the United States from the United Kingdom after the United States had attained independence than before.) The British immigrants were, on the average, better educated, better qualified technologically, and wealthier than newcomers from Eastern and Southern Europe. The British people who arrived in the United States did not regard themselves as a minority; their presence in the United States was regarded by the American White Anglo-Saxon Protestant (WASP) establishment as a welcome counterweight to assorted foreigners (mostly Catholic) from Eastern and Southern Europe, slightingly referred to as "dirty whites." The British immigrants helped offset the anti-British sentiment occasioned by the Civil War in the North and by a variety of lesser disputes between Britain and the United States over the Canadian boundary, fishery rights, and suchlike.

But WASP culture had dominated the United States from the seventeenth century on and shaped the American character, according to Richard Brookhiser in *The Way of the WASP* (1991). No immigrant group has yet been able to establish a rival way of life. The WASPs had political power, economic dominance, and social prestige. Their institutions were Ivy League schools, the Episcopal church, Wall Street, and the State Department. Although elitist, WASPs allowed people of character and intelligence to join. WASP values, claims Brookhiser, made America great, wealthy, and independent. The most important values were success due to hard work, civic-mindedness, antisensuality, and "conscience watching over everything." Immigrants to America were expected to adopt these values; they mostly did, and the country flourished as a result. The white Protestant establishment weakened after World War II and in the 1980s staggered under attacks from multiculturalism—a most unpleasant alternative to the WASPs' culture.

The United States was from its beginnings the immigrants' refuge par excellence. In this capacity the United States was far more significant than any other country, be it Australia, Brazil, Canada, or the Argentine. By contrast, few Americans sought permanent homes for themselves abroad, except a handful of blacks who went to Liberia, Finnish Americans who migrated to the Soviet Union, and a small number of American Jews who settled in Israel. But Americans of whatever race, color, or creed rarely changed their U.S. nationality. Overwhelmingly, they preferred real or alleged domestic ills to the putative advantages of foreign lands.

There were, of course, exceptions. Not all foreign-born immigrants to the United States remained in America; some went back to countries such as Britain, where there was no religious or racial persecution. The role of the returned American immigrant—British, German, Mexican, Italian, Greek, etc.—remains to be studied. Frequently he or she returned home with new ideas and some accumulated savings that enabled her or him to rise both socially and economically. In addition, American entrepreneurs, from the end of the last century, began to set up affiliates in Europe, especially in Britain, where U.S. firms such as Singer and Ford and discount stores such as Woolworth found no language barriers to impede their work. From Britain, American trusts often extended their operations to the British colonies and the European continent.

AMERICA IN THE GLOBAL ARENA

Relations between Britain and the United States improved in other ways, too. By the end of the last century, the British government stood resolved to avoid conflicts with its so-called American cousins at almost any cost. To Britain, imperial Germany with its great High Seas Fleet seemed an immeasurably greater menace than the United States. Hence, the British generally sympathized with the United States during the Spanish-American War of 1898. (Kipling's much-misquoted poem "Take Up the White Man's Burden" was written to encourage Americans in their imperial venture.)

The Spanish-American War formed another watershed in U.S. relations with foreign countries. Earlier wars fought by the United States had been confined to the North American land mass, had not involved transmaritime expansion, and had widened existing rifts within the U.S. electorate, pitting practitioners of American realpolitik against those who considered themselves godly. (For example, the Mexican-American War, 1846–1848, had been popular in the slave states, unpopular in New England.) The Spanish-

American War, by contrast, had more enthusiastic and united support from Americans than all previous and most subsequent wars engaging the United States. Chauvinists determined to teach objectionable Latins a lesson suddenly found themselves in thorough agreement with humanitarians determined to end Spanish imperialist oppression in Cuba. (There was, moreover, no Spanish ethnic lobby in the United States. Spaniards were more likely to emigrate to Latin America than to the United States, whereas Spanish Americans, including Mexican Americans, were more apt to side against Spain than with Spain.) Although the postwar annexation of the Philippines created bitter divisions, the campaign to expel the Spaniards from the New World met with almost universal approbation. America now stepped into the global arena with imperial ambitions and one of the world's major navies. The Spanish-American War thus inaugurated a revolutionary change in world affairs.

Fear of foreign entanglement was also weakened by the subsequent war in the Philippine Islands and American participation in the Boxer relief expedition to Beijing (1900)—actions unthinkable as late as 1884, when the U.S. Senate opposed sending observers to the Berlin conference to discuss African affairs, even though Americans were important traders and explorers in the region. When Theodore Roosevelt became president in 1901, he was determined that the United States should play a greater role in world affairs. And he saw to it that it did. Roosevelt was the most activist president in U.S. history until Woodrow Wilson. For example, in 1904 Roosevelt called a peace conference to end the Russo-Japanese war in order to maintain a power equilibrium in Asia. (The desire to maintain a balance of power was the principal reason for U.S. intervention against Germany in World Wars I and II.) At the Algeciras conference, called in 1906 to discuss Germany and France's quarrel over Morocco, Roosevelt even got the German kaiser to compromise.

Even more striking was the United States' economic impact overseas. From the 1870s onward, American farmers in the Middle West sent cargoes of grain and meat overseas; improved shipping and methods of refrigeration cheapened the costs of transport. European producers, including British aristocrats and Prussian

Junkers, found it increasingly difficult to comptete with Americans (and also Argentinians and Australians). As a manufacturing nation and as a producer of vital raw materials such as coal, iron, and steel, the United States began to overshadow the major European countries. (By 1914, the United States already turned out nearly five times as much steel as Britain and more than twice as much as the German Empire. The United States produced nearly three times as much pig iron as Britain and twice as much as Germany.)[14] The United States no longer fitted into the accepted framework of European great power relationships, a fact as yet unrecognized by most policymakers and theoreticians on both sides of the Atlantic. Yet American economic influence was beginning to be apparent, especially in Britain.[15]

How would Americans use this enormous might? When World War I started, the answer seemed clear: the Americans would not use this power at all but would stay clear of European entanglements. European affairs no longer seemed the business of a people whose forebears had left their native shores for good reasons and bad—to escape religious persecution, to avoid the draft, to escape poverty, to evade the unwelcome attention of tax gatherers, rent collectors, or wronged maidens. Public opinion regarding World War I was, moreover, divided along cleavages of class and ethnicity that remained characteristic of American politics. British Americans naturally sympathized with Britain's cause. The U.S. Eastern establishment—linked to the British upper class through ties of trade, education, and sometimes marriage—was also sympathetic and receptive to the claim that Britain represented the causes of parliamentary democracy and small nations. Danes and Norwegians tended to support the Western allies, as did Italians, Serbs, Czechs, and Romanians, who were generally hostile to the Hapsburg Empire allied to Germany.

But there was also substantial support for Germany. Swedes were often Germanophiles (unlike Danes and Norwegians). Subsequent Nazi stereotypes notwithstanding, Jews were apt to regard the German cause with sympathy and side with their former countrypeople. Yiddish-speakers from Eastern Europe found the pogrom-ridden czarist monarchy more objectionable than the German Empire, which did not persecute Jews and whose citizens spoke High German, a tongue closely linked to Yiddish. The Irish (about 4.5 million people) likewise formed a major bloc. To most Irish, any foe of Britain's seemed a friend. Moreover, the Irish, who, like the Italians and the Jews, had mainly settled in big cities along the Eastern seaboard, formed an influential lobby, powerful especially in municipal politics.

Above all, there was a substantial German minority: more than 8 million of America's 105 million people at the time had been born in Germany or had at least one German parent. The Germans, who were concentrated in the Middle West, had long been settled in the United States (one-tenth of the Union forces during the Civil War consisted of Germans). Germans as a group had done well in the United States. The German cultural influence, moreover, had been considerable. The United States was heavily indebted to German models for the structure of postgraduate training and for experts and expertise in a variety of academic disciplines: between 1815 and 1914 an estimated 9,000 to 10,000 Americans went to German universities. Germans were reputed to be thorough, hard-working, and sentimental. It was a time when loan words from the German language consisted only of such friendly sounding ones as *Lieder*, *Kindergarten*, and *Oktoberfest*—*Gestapo*, *Panzer*, and *Endlösung* were as yet unknown.

The strength of isolationist sentiment in the United States ensured that the country at first stayed neutral. But when imperial Germany began to conduct unrestricted warfare against Great Britain, the United States was drawn in. American lives were lost; American ships went to the bottom of the sea. To make matters worse, British intelligence caught Germans in a plot (revealed in the Zimmermann note) proposing an alliance between Germany, Mexico, and Japan if the United States went to war. Mexico would then recover the lost territory in Texas, New Mexico, and Arizona, which the United States had taken after winning the Mexican-American War. Ironically, imperial Germany's military victory over Russia—a feat never achieved by the Third Reich—worsened Germany's political condition. Once the Romanov dynasty fell, the Western allies' cause was no longer tainted by association with czarist absolutism; the allies' claim to be defending democracy seemed more credible than ever, not only to people of Anglo-Saxon stock but also to Jews, Poles, Balts, Finns, and other reluctant subjects of the former czars.

In 1917, the United States entered World War I. In military terms alone, the U.S. contribution was not as impressive as that of Britain or France. In economic and diplomatic terms, however, the contributions were unmistakable. President Woodrow Wilson issued his Fourteen Points (proclaiming the right of national self-determination) unilaterally; the United States had become the world's most productive economy. Having been an importer of capital, the United States switched to being an exporter. Without American financial support, Britain could not have continued the war effectively. By 1917 its gold reserves were virtually exhausted; most of its American assets had been sold. Even though Britain in 1918 commanded the world's largest navy, the largest air force, the greatest number of tanks, and the greatest colonial empire, it was American power that underpinned the alliance.

The global balance of power thereby underwent a decisive shift—one that German planners were slow to understand. For all the efficiency of their staff work, the Germans failed to grasp that the United States' economic potential now heavily outclassed that of any European power. Germany, whose priority should have been to keep the United States out of the war at any cost, instead gravely underestimated the Americans, a mistake that would continue to be made for generations to come. World War I also carried other lessons. Despite its internal divisions, the American Republic rested on much more solid foundations than its critics imagined. There was social unrest. But there was never, at any time, the slightest chance of a social revolution. Moreover, despite its multiethnic character, the United States developed none of the ethnic fissures that plagued the czarist, the Hapsburg, and later the Soviet empires.

True enough, the U.S. involvement in World War I led to an outbreak of anti-German hysteria, with vandalism, the public burning of German books, and the renaming of towns and even foods (frankfurters became hot dogs; German cabbage became liberty cabbage). The Germans in the United States encountered particular animosity for a time, for Germans were the only non-English-speaking immigrants who looked on their native country as an alternative model, as successful industrially, militarily, and culturally as the United States. The German lobby, moreover, was badly divided into Protestants and Catholics, "church Germans" and secularists, progressives (such as Governor John Peter Altgeld of Illinois), and conservatives. However, once the United States entered the war, German Americans remained loyal to their adopted country, and in time anti-German sentiment abated. Whatever political strength an ethnic lobby in the United States had, such a lobby would never be used as a fifth column on behalf of a foreign country.

Retreat from Europe

Having played a decisive part in the war, the United States might have been expected to dominate the peace. Instead, America once more retreated from Europe, disillusioned with "the war to end all wars." The United States would not join the League of Nations pioneered by President Wilson. His Fourteen Points were forgotten. ("Fourteen Points," scoffed Georges Clemenceau, the great French war leader, "ten were enough for the Almighty.") The United States refused to commit itself to future help for Europe; for instance, no guarantees were given France against future German aggression. There was contempt in Congress for those European countries (except Finland) that defaulted, wholly or in part, on their war debts.

Isolationism found expression in restrictions on immigration. (Those included a quota system, elaborated in 1924, which was designed to favor Northern Europeans against assorted Slavs, Latins, Greeks, Jews, and Turks. Chinese and Japanese were excluded altogether.) Isolationism also went with high tariffs (popular in particular with Republicans and embodied in legislation such as the Emergency Tariff Act of 1921). There was bitter hostility toward those suspected of having "gotten us into war." Critics derived from every part of the American political spectrum, including Midwestern Republicans who denounced Wall Street, the City (London's financial center), and an international cohort of arms manufacturers, the so-called merchants of death. It became almost a truism that the United States had gone to war to save the bankers and merchants who had strained themselves to the utmost to supply Britain and France with credit and arms. Isolationism was also reflected in U.S. defense policies. With its huge economic potential, the United States could easily have become the world's premier naval power. Instead, the United States, at the Washington Naval Conference (1922), settled for parity with Britain; the U.S. Air Force remained puny; and the U.S. Army was reduced to a size that could not have confronted even a minor European army, such as that of Belgium or Switzerland.

There was no effective political cooperation between the United States and its former allies after the war or during the Great Depression or during the rise of nazism. Despite American isolationism, however, U.S. cultural influence on Europe grew apace. Americans continued to come to Europe as tourists, performers, merchants, and students. American artists crossed the Atlantic, as did American prizefighters and American entertainers, especially black artists. Hollywood movies conquered the world—neither German UFA nor Sovfilm could compete on the world market with American studios. The mass-produced car, cheap enough for ordinary people to buy, seemed peculiarly American. (In Europe, by contrast, the automobile long remained the chosen vehicle of the rich.) Jazz was the Americans' music par excellence, no matter how loudly traditionalists objected; jazz triumphed in the dance halls and even affected classical music (as in Ernst Krenek's jazz opera [*Jonny spielt auf*]). American performers scored brilliant successes in the European capitals (even the Nazis, who denounced jazz as the decadent production of Negro and Jewish *Untermenschen*, had to permit modified forms of jazz at their receptions). Americans saw themselves as harbingers of modernity, mass culture, mass production, and mass consumption. Many European intellectuals shared these assumptions. "Skyscrapers," Jean Paul Sartre reflected, "were the architecture of the future, just as the cinema was the art and jazz the music of the future."[16] Meanwhile, American intellectuals bemoaned the fact that the United States had produced few great artists, musicians, or writers and depreciated America's cultural achievements. Not until the 1930s did some Americans begin to appreciate the richness of American culture. But it was the achievements of World War II that produced confidence, optimism, and a sense of America's greatness.

Then as now, of course, the traffic in ideas went both ways. Americans went to Europe to study German management methods, nuclear physics, and linguistics; German engineering; French art; British banking and maritime technology, as well as being Rhodes Scholars. Americans remained profoundly indebted to European pioneers in every field, from architecture to zoology. In music, even the saxophone, that quintessentially modern American jazz instrument, had been invented in Paris by Adolphe Sax, a contemporary of Richard Wagner's. All the same, the American contribution was in some ways unique and so was American economic power. By the mid-1920s, when the world economy had temporarily recovered from World War I, the United States had become the world's largest exporter and the principal source of new, as opposed to existing, capital investments. Roughly half America's new investments went to Europe, particularly Germany, where U.S. private investors for a time helped pay for reparations and for the funding of the Weimar Republic's welfare state. (Most of the war debt was never repaid.) It was a time when even the Communists, with all their dislike of Wall Street, had a soft spot for "Fordism," that specifically American combination of mass production methods and high wages.

Equally important later on was the impact of the New Deal. Despite pessimistic forecasts, American capitalism did not collapse as a result of the Great Depression; communism did not develop into a mass movement; fascism did not take root among Americans. (Most Italian Americans stood aloof from fascism; the great majority of German Americans had no sympathy for Hitler, whose followers in the United States, organized in the German-American Bund, never amounted to much.) The New Deal aroused widespread admiration in Europe among moderates, conservatives, Social Democrats, and Labour party supporters alike—America provided public works such as highways, dams, electrical projects, even mural art but without the militarism that accompanied such projects in totalitarian countries.

Europeans had other reasons for looking with favor at the United States. For all its restrictions on immigration, the United States remained by far the most open country in the world for people seeking refuge from nazi, fascist, and later communist oppression.

The newcomers during the 1930s, many of them Jewish or linked to Jews by ties of friendship or marriage, included famous scientists, actors, poets, novelists, filmmakers, physicians, and historians in one of the great intellectual migrations of European history. A goodly number came from Britain, but the bulk of them derived from German-speaking Central Europe, Poland, and the lands of the former Austro-Hungarian Empire.

The United States was now coming into its own in every sphere of intellectual endeavor. Up to 1933, when Hitler took over, Germany had always produced the largest number of Nobel Prize winners in medicine and the sciences. From then onward the balance of power irreversibly shifted; henceforth the United States always headed the list. U.S. predominance continued even after the European refugee scholars of the 1930s had begun to retire from their positions at U.S. universities. (Between 1957 and 1990 the United States gained 113 Nobel Prizes in the sciences and economics, as against 53 won by the European Community [EC] countries and 2 by Japan.) Not all the newcomers, of course, liked the United States or remained permanently; for example, Thomas Mann and Bertold Brecht returned to Europe after World War II. Nevertheless, the great migration strengthened existing intellectual ties between Europe and North America. American science, technology, and business methods and organizations had clearly reached world stature.

The United States also became involved in Europe's ideological struggles. To millions of Americans, the Spanish civil war (1936–39) in particular became a conflict between good and evil. No other foreign civil strife had ever aroused similar passions in America. The supporters of the Spanish Republic included not merely active Communists, a small but relatively influential group, but a broad alliance of moderate socialists, liberals, and self-styled progressive conservatives. To them, the war meant a crucial struggle against fascism worldwide—a view popularized not only by Ernest Hemingway and leftist intellectuals but also, later, by popular movie personalities such as Ingrid Bergman in *For Whom the Bell Tolls*. Franco supporters were less numerous but also influential. They derived not so much from declared Fascists but from militant anti-Communists and Catholics aghast at the persecution of nuns and priests at the "reds'" behest. Several thousand Americans departed to fight in Spain with the Loyalists in the Abraham Lincoln Brigade; to most American intellectuals the Spanish civil war henceforth provided a mirror in which world events would continue to be reflected—with progress forever arrayed against reaction, vice against virtue, capitalism against socialism.

Nevertheless, the bulk of the American people remained neutralist. However much professors and journalists might argue about the Spanish civil war or nazism in Germany or Stalinism in Russia, the mass of the U.S. population wished to remain uninvolved. Once World War II started in Europe, however, the Allied cause aroused sympathy among the great majority of Americans. But despite President Roosevelt's endeavors (Lend-Lease Act, 1941) and the Anglophilia of the old East Coast establishment, the United States would probably not have entered all-out war but for Japan's attack on Pearl Harbor on December 7, 1941, and Germany's declaration of war against the United States.

RETURN TO EUROPE

Yet once having stepped into the arena, the Americans meant to win—with a resolve never grasped by either German or Japanese policymakers. The United States rejected an "Asia First" strategy advocated by traditional isolationists and instead concentrated its main efforts against Hitler, who was correctly perceived as the main enemy. The immense resources of the United States proved decisive in winning the war. After Pearl Harbor, there was in the United States a political unanimity not witnessed again until the gulf war fifty years later. American society, though ethnically mixed, displayed its accustomed cohesion during World War II. German Americans, Italian Americans, Japanese Americans overwhelmingly proved loyal. The American way of life made a strong appeal even to German prisoners of war in the United States. (There were something like 400,000 of them, as against only 50,000 Italians; of a selected sample of those returning to Germany, 74 percent left with friendly feelings toward the United States. They included men of subsequent prominence in the Federal Republic of Germany.)

American private enterprise, though controlled and restricted by extensive governmental regulation, staged a miracle of mobilization never previously seen in world history. Big science came into its own, financed with huge public grants, linked to the universities and to a massive industrial complex. The American fleet became the world's mightiest—as if Pearl Harbor had never occurred. The U.S. Air Force came to dominate the skies. No one who ever saw the giant air armadas that filled the sky during the invasion of Normandy will ever forget the sight, a shattering display of American or American-subsidized British air power. The United States deployed the greatest army ever sent overseas in world history. The GI's were better dressed, better paid, and more expansively equipped than any European soldiers. In the European imagination the olive-uniformed Yanks—tall, gangling, gum-chewing—appeared astonishing in their self-confidence. British soldiers might resent the Yanks' superior pay and their reputation for courting British women with perfume and silk stockings unavailable in British shops. But though he might scoff at the Americans, Tommy Atkins (Britain's GI Joe) was glad at heart that the Yanks had come. The United States had been the "arsenal of democracy," and this the Allies appreciated.

The American army, moreover, seemed more democratic than European armies. There were no separate sergeants' messes in the U.S. Army, as there were in the British army; proportionately more U.S. enlisted men became officers than in the British army. Americans performed impressively, especially at tasks requiring engineering skills or complex organization of the kind involved in seaborne landings. Germans soldiers might taunt the Americans for their initial inexperience or lack of discipline. But members of the Wehrmacht were impressed by the massive weight of firepower that Americans could deploy and their ability to learn fast from previous errors. Every German soldier would infinitely sooner be taken prisoner by the Americans than by the Russians or even the French; to be sent to a prisoner-of-war camp in the United States was accounted a first prize in the Wehrmacht's lottery of defeat. Above all, once the fighting stopped, Germans without exception preferred to dwell in the American than the Soviet zone of occupation.

The Americans also consolidated their economic supremacy. Whereas much of Europe had suffered devastation on an unparalleled scale, the American homeland witnessed an extraordinary growth of American industrial productivity and an unprecedented rise in the gross national product (from $11.0 billion, in 1929 prices, in 1939 to $180.9 billion in 1945). For many Americans, the war—despite its hardships and dangers—turned into a positive experience, creating an almost universal labor shortage, which meant that wages rose and that formerly unemployed workers had money to spend on luxuries as well as necessities. Millions of black Americans migrated North and found jobs in industry that had formerly been denied to them. Hostility, education and job discrimination against Catholics and Jews diminished. Millions of women moved into the labor force; many of them stayed in their newfound posts after the war, with the result that five million more women were in paid employment by 1946 than in 1941. In the United States, at war's end prosperity created new expectations and overall a new sense of optimism and well-being.

By their joint exertions, the United States and Britain restored the prestige of democratic government, badly tarnished during the 1930s when nazism and fascism had appeared to be the wave of the future. American society and the American economy worked. The international effect of U.S. (and British) democracy was enormous. Unlike Hitler, Mussolini, and Stalin, neither Roosevelt nor Churchill feared plots from their generals. American society—based on a modified free enterprise principle—created a productive miracle that would have appeared improbable even to writers of science fiction. The American and British alone had a credible record of maintaining civil liberty. (The internment of Japanese Americans in the United States and of many German Jewish refugees in Great Britain was a regrettable departure from the Allies' high standards; however, the civilian prisoners in every other belligerent country—Germany, Japan, France, the Soviet Union—would have gladly traded places with those in Anglo-American hands.)

World War II was likewise decisive in shaping future relations between the United States and its Western Allies. President Roosevelt's great design (the Atlantic Charter) differed much from what later transpired. Roosevelt believed that there could be a permanent partnership between the United States and the Soviet Union. Treated with consideration, granted its rightful sphere of influence in Eastern Europe, the Soviet Union would collaborate with Western capitalism in a new world order. This would be run through the United Nations but would be essentially based on a partnership between the "Big Four"—the United States, the Soviet Union, China, and Britain. Relations with Britain would be friendly, but the British, as well as the French and the Dutch, would have to surrender their ill-gotten empires in the cause of world peace.

In fact there was friction between the United States and the Soviet Union during the war. By contrast, U.S. ties with Britain (and the so-called white Dominions, Canada, Australia, New Zealand, South Africa), were infinitely tighter than with any other country. U.S. and British diplomatists might disagree over Soviet ambitions or the future of the British Empire; U.S. and British strategists might quarrel over the impending invasion of the European continent; U.S. and British sailors would customarily get into fights when going ashore in the same port. But U.S. and British economic and defense policies were much more closely coordinated than those of any sovereign allies. This special relationship remains just as real fifty years later.[17]

Relations with France, by contrast, were much worse—and remained so for years to come. Roosevelt personally disliked Charles de Gaulle, France's wartime leader. Indeed, the two stood worlds apart. De Gaulle was a proud and touchy soldier, a believer in realpolitik, intensely preoccupied with his country's prestige, sure that he alone embodied his country's glory and esprit. Roosevelt, intensely civilian in his ethos, never awed by martial splendor, was convinced that the United States should guide the world into a new moral order that would supersede old world power politics. Roosevelt refused to regard de Gaulle as France's only legitimate representative. Roosevelt, moreover, always projected domestic politics on the foreign screen; there was no French voting lobby in the United States, as there was a Polish, an Irish, and a Jewish lobby. French interests thus were held of small account.

U.S. relations with Italy, oddly enough, were easier. The German alliance was unpopular in Italy; Mussolini's much-heralded "pact of steel" with Hitler would never have survived a popular referendum. Once the Allies were firmly entrenched in Italy and Germany's defeat seemed certain, Mussolini fell and Italy switched sides. The

Italians cooperated with the Allies, and the United States began to render massive aid to its former enemy, a policy welcomed with special enthusiasm by Italian Americans, by Catholics of all ethnic backgrounds, and by other enemies of Stalinism who feared the challenge posed by the powerful Italian Communist party.

U.S. opinion regarding Germany was much more complex. After World War I, there had arisen a feeling of guilt among many intellectuals, a sense that Germany had been victimized by allied rapacity in the Treaty of Versailles (1919). There was no such pro-Germanism after World War II—the Nazis, with their murderous campaigns and death camps, had too grossly besmirched their country's reputation. Indeed it was intellectually fashionable to be hostile to Germany; sophisticates who would have blanched at expressing the slightest hostility to Jews or blacks could indulge in anti-German remarks to their heart's content. Nevertheless, anti-Germanism in the United States never became as powerful as it did for a time in Britain during World War II, when leading intellectuals such as A. J. P. Taylor, Sir Lewis Namier, and Hugh Dalton became vigorous proponents of anti-Germanism. The United States, by contrast, never felt in mortal danger of Germany; about one-fifth of the U.S. population traced their descent wholly or partly to Germany. German names such as Eisenhower, Spaatz, and Nimitz were conspicuous among the list of the United States' greatest commanders; the German impact was profound on the Lutheran churches and, to a lesser extent, on the Catholic church. Once the war had ended and the Morgenthau plan to reduce Germany to a "potato patch" was seen to be a blunder, there was little doubt that a reformed and repentant Germany would work its way back into American esteem. West Germany came to be seen as the dynamo for restructuring Europe and as the shield, with U.S. help, against Soviet might.

World War II was also fraught with other far-reaching consequences. Americans became convinced that only a united Europe free of economic nationalism, trade wars, and custom duties would prevent future European wars; the United States should constitute a model for Europeans to follow. A political federation, however, would only work if sustained by a prosperous and expanding economy. Hence U.S. policymakers became convinced, during the war, that the United States must provide financial aid and that the New

Deal should be exported to Europe. The Atlantic Charter, the Four Freedoms, Lend Lease all reflected the Americans' new spirit of humanitarian interventionism.

By contrast, there was in Europe, when the war ended, a pervasive pessimism expressed in gloomy philosophies such as existentialism. Entire cities lay in ruins, millions of people had lost their lives in battle, in bombing, or in death camps. To return even to prewar normalcy seemed for many Europeans an unattainable fantasy. Compared with the Europeans' pessimism, the Americans had a healthy optimism. The Americans' belief in economic growth, in a dynamic society sustained by mass production, in mass consumption, and in social equality provided that element of hope that would prove essential for Europe's postwar recovery.[18]

America also continued to influence Europe's popular culture. Jazz remained a major contribution of black Americans. U.S. popular music also derived inspiration from the traditional strains of the American West (themselves influenced by Mexican *corridos*, or ballads) and from tunes brought across the Atlantic by European immigrants—English, Irish, German, Jewish, Italian, and others. American music in turn spread through the remotest parts of the globe; musicians such as Bing Crosby and Louis Armstrong were acclaimed as much abroad as at home. Also acclaimed were American movies, some of which were fantasies that spread disinformation concerning the real America. American movies and musical comedies similarly supplied much of Europe's entertainment; all modern fairy-tale characters—Superman, Donald Duck, Bambi, the Wizard of Oz, the heroic cowboy—came from America.

To the old-style European liberal, the United States was the bastion of freedom. To the refugee scientist of the 1930s, the United States provided new academic opportunities as well as shelter. To social reformers (including British Labourites such as Ernest Bevin and Harold Laski), the United States was the land of the New Deal. To the efficiency expert, the United States was the country that pioneered mass production methods. America was also the land in which a person might redeem failures suffered in the old country. Alternatively, the "rich uncle from America" appeared in melodrama as a deus ex machina, ready to help an ambitious young man in his career. (This theme returned in the 1980s in *Heimat*, an enormously popular German television series.) And even critics of the United States such as Bertrand Russell or Arnold Toynbee never hesitated privately to make money in a country they denigrated in public.

The United States dominated not only Europe but the world. The United States held a temporary monopoly of nuclear arms. It stood supreme in the natural and physical sciences. In religious terms regarding the number of practicing believers and trained personnel and financial resources, the United States was at once the world's largest Protestant, Catholic, and Jewish country. America contributed more to international charity than the rest of the world combined: terms such as "Joint" and "Care" packages entered the international vocabulary. Even international bodies such as the United Nations Relief and Rehabilitation Administration (UNRRA) were largely financed with the American taxpayers' money.

Overall, American English came to be what Latin had been to the literate classes of medieval Europe—the principal language of international communications as well as a prestige symbol. (The use of English spread through textbooks, teacher exchanges, student travel, tourism, imported films, television programs, and jazz and through English terminology in international organizations, banking, aviation, maritime communications, and the military. English also dominated in the social sciences and scientific and technological publications.) The role of English became particularly important in smaller countries such as Sweden and Holland; neither French nor German could equal the importance of English throughout Europe and the world at large. American broadcasts also had tremendous political influence. Few Americans realize the enormous impact that the Voice of America, Radio Free Europe, and Radio Liberty (beamed to the Soviet Union) had on the Soviet satellites.[19]

The United States moreover enjoyed special advantages with regard to its civic culture. The U.S. Constitution of 1787 is the world's oldest written constitution and has helped make the United States one of the most politically stable countries in the world. (Even during the stormy 1960s, hardly any revolutionary professed a willingness to abolish the Constitution, however much he or she expressed hostility to the hated "system" in general.) The American Constitution was studied with interest by the founding fathers of the German Federal Republic and the Italian Republic after World War

II and later by scholars and politicians during the Soviet Union's demise. The *Federalist Papers* would remain relevant when the works of Lenin and Stalin were moldering in the attic. American federalism, the system of checks and balances, of the separation of powers, has been modified but has endured and remained a strength of American democracy. No Marxist-inspired constitution could make a similar claim. And European Community enthusiasts speak of a federal union of nations to form a United States of Europe.

At the same time the United States enjoyed a high level of interest in politics, media attention to political affairs, pride in the country, a sense of civic duty, and trust in political institutions. American constitutionalism helped integrate wave after wave of immigrants into the U.S. political culture. Up to the late 1960s, U.S. respondents in public opinion polls thought more highly about their own political system and displayed more participatory and supportive attitudes than non-Americans. Americans, on the whole, also felt more certain of their ability to influence governmental action than most Europeans. Not surprisingly, the United States after World War II saw itself as the major actor in world history.

The partial Americanization of Europe had begun in wartime and continued after 1945. The United States, as the "arsenal of democracy," had equipped its Allies and provided the majority of forces for the war in the West and in the Pacific. Millions of troops had been stationed first in Britain, then in occupied Western Europe. Americans brought new habits, attitudes, and diets to Europeans. Mores and morals became more open and friendly and less class biased. Thousands of GI brides linked families across the Atlantic; sexual liaisons numbered in the millions. The GI's brought new ambition and appetites to help break down national stereotypes. Military governments ruled West Germany, Austria, and Italy, reshaped their governments, and helped liberalize their education systems and economies. The Marshall Plan (1947–51) was set up to revitalize Western Europe, and the North Atlantic Treaty Organization (NATO) was put together to defend the region against the threats of communism and Germany. The United States had truly come into its own; as Churchill noted at war's end, "America stands at this moment at the summit of the world."

Attitudes within the Atlantic Community after 1945

What of the attitudes within the Atlantic community as it evolved between the end of World War II and the 1980s? On both sides of the Atlantic there remained a good deal of ambivalence. Anti-Americanism continued to be influential—much of it reactionary and antimodern. Americans were resented for their political and economic power, their bragging, and their riches. America was identified with the real or imagined evils alike of urbanism and free enterprise. Some Europeans were envious and resentful of the United States. The British Labour party, according to Anthony Crosland, resented the United States because it took over leadership from the British and because of the success of capitalism over socialism. Certain British and European conservatives were anti-American because of the U.S. role in encouraging decolonization. (The 1956 Suez crisis was the most serious clash between European colonialism and American anticolonialism.)[20] Western Europe's dependency on the United States was another source of anguish and resentment. The United States not only helped Europe recover but also defended it against the Soviet Union. Dependency hurt some Europeans' pride but helped push them into working toward a United States of Europe to stand as a third force between the United States and the USSR.

The partial Americanization of Europe was somewhat balanced by the increasing influence of Europe on America. The ordinary immigrant from Western Europe was no longer an unskilled or semiskilled worker or farmer, as he or she had been in the olden days. The bulk of European newcomers were highly skilled technicians or professionals. European professors lectured at U.S. universities; European scientists worked at U.S. institutes. European investors played a major part in U.S. economic life. In terms of acquiring business assets in the United States, British, German, French, and Dutch investors between them played a much more important role than the much-discussed Japanese. There was ever-increasing cooperation between major corporations in the United States and Europe. For example, Daimler-Benz, a German giant, collaborated with U.S. corporations such as Westinghouse in manufacturing machinery required for mass transit, including engines for subways and automated train control components. Daimler subsidiaries manufactured heavy-duty trucks in the United States or turned out medical equipment. Indeed, Daimler's activities in the United States became so complex that the company had to open an office in Washington, D.C., just to handle relations with the U.S. government. As Daimler's chairman put it, "collaboration *sans frontières* is more and more becoming an indispensable prerequisite for one's own economic and technological success."[21]

Europe also influenced day-to-day living in the United States to an extent not understood by professional anti-Americans, who believed that cultural influence was a one-way street. An American executive might wake up to the buzz of a German-made Braun alarm clock, prepare Italian espresso in a German-manufactured Krups coffee maker, eat a croissant from the French-owned Vie de France bakery chain, spread butter supplied by the Anglo-Dutch Lever Group, purchased at a Giant supermarket owned by the Dutch Alber Hejn Group. Thus refreshed, the executive would have a hot shower with the new Lever 2000 soap, shave with a Norelco shaver from Philips, then slip into an Italian-made suit from Giorgio Armani. Thereafter he might ride to the office in a Swedish Volvo filled with gas at a BP (British Petroleum) station, pick up a Spanish business associate at the Watergate Hotel (owned by the British Trusthouse Forte Company), and discuss a new best-seller published by Doubleday (just acquired by the German firm of Bertelsmann). *C'est la vie.*

The United States and Europe also came to resemble one another in more fundamental ways. American life became much more bureaucratized than in the olden days; U.S. bureaucracies rivaled their European counterparts in arrogance and complexity. At the same time, the U.S. intelligentsia assumed a much more prominent place in U.S. life than two generations earlier—a development already familiar to Europeans.

Still, to nationalists in Europe, the United States was the dominant player in world politics, and the Europeans had to depend on the Americans for their military defense until the collapse of the Warsaw Pact in 1989. In the twenty-first century the Europeans may become the world's economic leaders, but they have yet to prove that they have military and political power equal to the United States or indeed that they can act forcefully as a political unit.[22]

Charges of economic imperialism were hurled at the United States throughout the postwar decades. Although the United States saw itself as an anticolonial power, leftists defined the United States as imperialistic because of its economic penetration of world markets. Lenin (*Imperialism*, 1917) defined imperialism as the last stage of capitalism; he thus made the United States appear as an imperialist power even though it had no colonies. West German leftist youths claimed that the United States had colonized Germany. The French had long preached against the American challenge, and the British left widely accepted the Marxist definition of the United States as a neocolonialist power. Opposition to American economic takeovers therefore was widespread in Europe from 1945 on; the European Economic Community (EEC) adopted a partially protectionist policy in 1958, and American multinationals who set up plants in Europe were perceived by Jean Louis Servan-Schreiber as embodiments of *The American Challenge* (first published in French in 1967).

American self-criticism was the source of much of this anti-Americanism in Europe. The attacks on American society by American liberal-left academics and journalists focused on the failures of capitalism, on the industrial-military complex, on civil rights abuses, and on the policy of containment. Critics such as Paul Baran, Noam Chomsky, Herbert Marcuse, Vance Packard, and Susan Sontag helped convince many Europeans of America's evil. Naive actresses such as Jane Fonda and Shirley MacLaine or Communist party functionaries such as Angela Davis were believed when they fantasized about American society. American newspaper columnists were among the worst America-bashers. Walter Lippmann kept saying that the cold war was America's fault. Anthony Lewis claimed that the United States was the most dangerous and destructive power in the world, and Tom Wicker claimed in the 1980s that the American system did not work—this at a time of the greatest prosperity and military power in the country's history.[23]

Much anti-Americanism in postwar Europe therefore was reinforced by American movies, television, drama, and popular music, for these all too often display only the worst aspects of American society—its criminality, racism, and violence. Nevertheless, many Americans found it hard to understand why, having saved Europe from self-destruction in World Wars I and II at great loss of American lives and having then helped rebuild that region after World War II, they were resented and treated with distrust.

Given the murderous history of communism, there could be no objective justification for treating the United States and the USSR as moral equivalents. Nevertheless, many European and U.S. intellectuals seldom stopped criticizing the United States, while excusing communism's failures. Some church officials even claimed that communism was morally superior to capitalism. Luckily, anti-Americanism never forced the United States to retreat into isolation or a "fortress America" mentality. The United States remained committed to NATO and globally containing communist expansion—not always with success.

Until the Vietnam War, the majority of Europeans liked the United States and believed it was seriously committed to their security. Thereafter, European distrust of U.S. leadership and judgment increased. Public opinion polls in Western Europe from 1954 to 1982 were generally more favorable than unfavorable to the United States but suspicious of U.S. political judgment.

There was also concern by scholars such as Paul Kennedy (The Rise and Fall of Great Powers, 1987) about the U.S. commitment to be the world's police force and U.S. ability to sustain its military status as a superpower. The United States supposedly had overreached itself by spending too much on defense at a time when the U.S. economy suffered from slow growth, a loss of technical superiority in many fields, national budget deficits, a trade deficit, and the poor education obtained by so many American high school students. Above all, the United States encountered criticism from the peace movements and the various Green parties, which censured the U.S. policy of nuclear deterrence. There was bitter resentment concerning the arms buildup initiated by President Carter and accelerated by President Reagan. Stephen Haseler has best summed up the nature of European anti-Americanism as not just opposition to U.S. policies but resentment of U.S. power and material success and a feeling of dependency on this superpower.

In the postwar period, many of Europe's elites believed that American democracy was without real culture and was excessively individualistic. The United States incurred censure at the same time for being vulgar and elitist, bellicose and soft, materialistic yet preachy. Anti-Americanism appealed to those who equated the United States with modernity in its worst aspects—with the destruction of customary family and religious ties. But the United States also was blamed for failing to develop the Third World in an adequate manner, for hogging too many of the world's resources. Anti-Americanism pleased nationalists of every description, who denigrated the United States as a collection of rootless cosmopolitans drawn from every nation on earth. But then the United States was also lambasted for its real or assumed chauvinism. Anti-Americanism frequently went with hostility to the Americans' capitalist ruthlessness. Yet U.S. capitalists were also denounced for their alleged inability to compete on the world market against Japanese and German competition.

Anti-Americanism appealed in particular to social elites—not so much the traditional upper classes but to leftist television producers, journalists, academics, clergy. They took pride not merely in their assumed superior intellectual ability but also in their social and aesthetic chic. Hence they widely enjoyed sneering at President Reagan as a former B-movie actor and at Prime Minister Thatcher for being a grocer's daughter from Grantham who bought her clothes at Marks and Spencer's (the British equivalent of Macy's). An American variant of this creed particularly blamed the WASPs. Thus Charles Reich's *The Greening of America* (1970) claimed that Americans found work empty, pointless, and enslaving, lampooning the WASPs with special severity. The political traditions of the American bourgeoisie were widely regarded with contempt; political freedom, personal liberty, limited government were exposed to ridicule. By contrast, now-discredited revolutionaries such as Fidel Castro and Che Guevara were held up for emulation.

From the late 1970s on, the intellectual configuration of the Western world began to change. By that time the prestige of communism was on the decline; only a handful of true believers and revolutionary theologians considered that communism represented a superior morality and superior economic efficiency. Not that anti-

Americanism ended. The United States did have worse crime and drug problems than any Western European country. A new breed of European right-wingers resented the United States as the homeland of feminism, multiculturalism, and other real or reputed cultural ills. There was also, from the 1980s onward, a new form of anti-Americanism inconceivable thirty years earlier—the equation of the United States with inefficient management, shoddy workmanship, and economic decline à l'anglaise. Exaggerated as those impressions might be, they derived in part from genuine deficiencies and also from grave errors in public relations. (It was surely one of President Bush's major errors to take, on an official trip to Japan, twenty-one corporate executives—including a senior official from General Motors who had just announced the layoff of 74,000 workers, the closing of numerous plants, and, in the bargain, an $80 million compensation package for the upper echelon of management.)[24]

Above all there was anti-Americanism homemade. Few foreigners ever denounced the United States with the same passion as Paul Fussell, an American writer to whom the United States was BAD, in capital letters, and hell was other Americans.[25] Such sentiments widely appealed to a moral coalition whose members drew their inspiration from three separate traditions—religious (particularly Quakers, Unitarians, Episcopalians, Jews); secular humanist (both Marxist and non-Marxist); and bohemian (including outsiders of every kind who gloried in their own alienation from society). Overwhelmingly they rejected the doctrine of original sin; they repudiated the past and put their trust into a glorious future. Whatever their philosophical antecedents, they regarded themselves—like seventeenth-century Puritans—as a chosen band, a moral vanguard, destined to lead the oppressed masses from present-day America, the new Egypt, to a promised land of the vanguard's own creation.

The impact of anti-Americanism, however, should not be exaggerated. The history of the Atlantic Community since the end of 1945 had, after all, been an extraordinary success story, at least for that part of Western Europe that, as the British *Economist* put it, had been "lucky enough to have been liberated (or defeated) by the Americans." Whereas the first part of the present century had been a time of disaster, the second had seen a period of peace unmatched since the post-Napoleonic era. "The average West European's income (at 1990 prices) has risen more than 300 percent from $4,860 a year in 1950 to $20,880 in 1990. Life expectancy for West Europeans went up in that time from 67 to 76 years."[26]

True enough, both Western Europe and the United States suffered from serious social problems. In Western Europe there were, for example, new ethnic tensions, as Western Europe became a magnet for immigrants. By 1992 the share of foreign-born people in many Western European countries was indeed higher than in the United States, the world's classic country of refuge. (In 1991 the share of foreign-born persons amounted to about 17 percent in Switzerland, 11 percent in France, 9 percent in Belgium, 7.5 percent in Germany, 6.3 percent in Britain as against 6 percent in the United States.) Of course no European country could compare with the United States as regards ethnic diversity. The United States in particular continued to suffer from bitter racial rivalries, as expressed, for example, in the 1992 riots in Los Angeles. Nevertheless, the United States' problems seem manageable when compared with those of other multiethnic countries such as Russia, Romania, Yugoslavia, and many others. Europeans widely appreciated America's relative tranquillity. Within the United States the moral coalition proved unexpectedly fissiparous as militant feminists, ecologists, gays, and minority advocates increasingly pursued divergent aims. The moral coalition could not easily gain a mass following in a country whose citizens, in public opinion polls, overwhelmingly expressed satisfaction with their own lives. (The same generalization applies to Western Europe.)

The breakdown of communism in the former Warsaw Pact countries weakened anti-Americanism both directly and indirectly. The enormous propaganda campaign directed and financed by the Soviet Union and its allies suddenly ceased. Marxists of every kind were suddenly put on the defensive. Why had they failed to foresee communism's impending disaster? Why had they so widely failed to understand the demographic, moral, and economic ravages experienced by every country that had ever been under communist rule? Moreover, by the 1980s, even before the breakup of the Soviet Union, some of the old-fashioned anti-Americanism of the French left had lost its sting. Jean-Paul Sartre, once the country's most influential intellectual, and anti-Americanism, once de rigueur among the smart set, became passé. From the 1980s onward it became acceptable among the literati to talk of *la France qui gagne* (the France that makes money), to appear preppy (*bon chic, bon genre*), and even to praise wines from California. As Richard Bernstein put it, "the noisome, Sartrean, fashionably leftist jargon that treated the United States as a bourgeois and therefore philistine tyranny, an 'imperialist' menace posing a threat at least as grave as the one posed by the Soviet Union has become *ringard* (fusty, old fashioned in French youth jargon)."[27]

As regards the future, the news is both bad and good. The United States and the Western European countries share comparable social problems. Voters in most Western countries faced rising rates of taxation, budget deficits, rising costs of social services, and dissatisfaction with the public services states were meant to deliver. In the United States, as in Europe, television dominated popular leisure. Religious attendance had widely diminished, and traditional values were in decline. Unemployment had turned into a pervasive problem, though generally worse in Western Europe than in the United States. Both Europeans and Americans were forced to adjust to a world where manufacturing industries required far fewer workers than in the past, a world where job opportunities for the unskilled, the semiskilled, and the archaically skilled kept diminishing. On both sides of the Atlantic the number of children born out of wedlock has greatly increased since the 1960s; it was 25 percent in the United States in 1993. In the United States the illegitimacy rate for whites now nearly equals the black rate of the mid-1960s, when scholars such as Daniel Patrick Moynihan first sounded the alarm over the decline of the black family.[28] But in Western Europe too the traditional family structure has weakened: the percentage of women-headed families has gone up and with it, drug consumption, crime (especially juvenile crime), and the feminization of poverty. Western Europe, like the United States, must cope with massive immigration and the resultant ethnic hostilities. In dealing with these and associated problems, Americans and Europeans can profit by learning from one another's experiences.

The breakdown of traditional authority has also affected politics on both sides of the Atlantic. Forty years ago, an Irish workman in a big American industrial city was likely to vote for the Democratic party, attend a Catholic church, and loyally support his union. A Welsh miner would probably vote for the Labour party, attend chapel, and likewise take pride in being a union man. A Bavarian woman would in all likelihood support the Christian Democratic party and go to mass. By contrast, a Walloon steelworker in Belgium would probably be a loyal socialist in politics and an agnostic in religion; in all likelihood, he would make sure that his daughter voted socialist and married a socialist.

By the 1990s, these certainties had greatly weakened. Political allegiances had become more fluid than in previous generations. Governing parties were in trouble all over the Atlantic Community. Besmirched by scandal, the Christian Democratic (CD) party in Italy had abdicated its leadership, which derived from the CD's opposition to the once-powerful Italian Communist party. The cold war having ended, Italian voters now feared the Mafia much more than the communists, and the Italian judicature had begun a revolutionary assault against Italy's former "political class." In France, the Socialist party had, by 1994, been reduced to a shadow of its former self. In Germany, confidence in the three main political parties had diminished. In Canada the ruling Progressive Conservative party had been shattered in the 1993 election. In the United States, the two major parties were riddled by internal disputes over issues such as health care, conservation, and the adoption of the North American Free Trade Agreement (NAFTA) in 1993. On both sides of the Atlantic ethnic and regional differences had widened within many countries—this at a time when the Soviet threat from without had gone. In the United States political arena there were heightened tensions between whites and blacks, gays and straights, feminists and traditionalists. Outside the United States regional loyalties had gained strength in countries as diverse as Belgium, Spain, Italy, and France. (A French cartoon showed two Frenchmen in conversation. "I am a xenophobe," proclaims the first. "Of which region?" asks the second.) Worse off still was Yugoslavia, which had turned into a European Lebanon.

But the good news outweighed the bad. The Soviet Empire had joined the former Western colonial empires in oblivion. The cold war ended. A "hot war" seemed so unlikely that all NATO members reduced their armed forces. The psychological impact of decommunization meant that all over Europe, East and West, former Marxist-Leninists were revising their resumés. Nobody had ever heard anything, seen anything, said anything, known anything, except for handful of oldsters now on sickbeds, in their dotage, or in exile. Communism had ended not with a bang but with a whimper. Academic Marxism was in the doldrums in every Western country except the United States, where left-wingers had been less exposed to the practice of "real existing socialism" than their colleagues in the formerly communist countries.

Diplomatic relations between the United States and its Western European allies were remarkably good. Unlike Britain and France, the United States had not attempted to place obstacles in the way of German reunification. Germany remained Washington's principal ally in Europe, as well as a major trading partner. U.S.-British relations did not remain as close under President Clinton as they had been under President Bush and even more so under President Reagan. In President Reagan's day, admiration for Margaret Thatcher nearly equaled the respect paid to Winston Churchill in World War II. Nevertheless, President Clinton took pride in being an Oxford man, and no major issues divided the two countries. No matter what theoreticians might say, a "special relationship" continued to link the United States with Britain and Ireland, the only two European countries where United States tourists could feel at home without having to learn a new language. Franco-American relations suffered from disputes over tariffs (especially those concerned with U.S. farming imports and U.S. movies). But again, there were no major disputes over principles. The visceral anti-Americanism of Jean-Paul Sartre's day had disappeared. On the contrary, a reputed familiarity with the writings of Milton Friedman had become politically acceptable. To be a connoisseur of California wines was definitely chic. Spain's democracy had turned out to be a striking success, and no one asked—as many scholars did in the 1970s—whether it would last. The Portuguese dictatorship had become a remote memory. Franco-German, Anglo-French, or Anglo-German wars of earlier years had come to seem light years away. The United States, it was widely believed, would never again have to be involved in intra-European conflicts.

The United States was also bound to benefit from the EC's creation of a single market (finalized in 1993). The EC stands out as one of the United States' chief trading partners, and the United States seems bound to profit from the EC's transformation into a single market—with freedom for people, capital, and services to move within the EC's border. The United States also is a model for those European federalists who aim at turning the EC into a United States of Europe. (The Maastricht Treaty, put into force in 1993, indeed looked to a superfederation with a uniform currency, a joint foreign and security policy, and a common social charter.) In our opinion, those goals are unattainable, and the United States has little interest in supporting them. No matter what constitutional lawyers might say, effective sovereignty in the EC would continue to rest with the constituent states—not the federal power, as it does in the United States. The reason for that state of affairs is simple: the EC is a union of twelve diverse states with different languages and cultures. If push came to shove, the EC would never go to war to prevent one of its member states from seceding—unlike the United States in the Civil War, the Swiss Confederation in the so-called *Sonderbundskrieg*, or Nigeria in the civil conflict against Ibo secessionists. The United States in future would have to accept Western Europe for what it was and what it remains—an association of states linked both to one another and to the United States by ties of history, commerce, and a common culture. Given the state of Europe fifty years ago, this is indeed a mighty change for the better. The Western world truly has cause to be grateful.

Notes

1. Page Smith, *Trial by Fire: A People's History of the Civil War and Reconstruction* (New York, Penguin Books, 1990), p. 29.
2. See Peter Duignan and L. H. Gann, *The Rebirth of the West: The Americanization of the Democratic World, 1945–1958* (Oxford, Eng.: Blackwell, 1992).
3. Mark P. Lagon and Michel Lind, "American Way: The Enduring Interests of U. S. Foreign Policy," *Policy Review*, Summer 1991, pp. 38–44. See also Peter Duignan and L. H. Gann, *The United States and Africa: A History* (New York: Cambridge University Press, 1984), chap. 5.
4. Alexis de Tocqueville, *Democracy in America*, ed. J. P. Mayer (Garden City, N.Y.: Doubleday, 1969), p. 33. See also Daniel J. Boorstin, *America and the Image of Europe* (New York: World Publishing, 1964).
5. "An American," *Collected Verse of Rudyard Kipling* (New York: Doubleday, 1910), pp. 97–99.
6. Nathan Glazer, "The Structure of Ethnicity," *Public Opinion*, October–November 1984, pp. 2–5.
7. Cited respectively from Pierre Berton, *The Invasion of Canada, 1812–1813* (Ontario: Penguin Books, 1988), p. 42, and Arthur Hertzberg, *The Jews in America: Four Centuries of an Uneasy Encounter* (New York: Simon and Schuster, 1989), p. 157.
8. Leo Schelbert and Hedwing Rappold, eds, *Alles ist ganz anders hier: Auswanderer-Schicksale in Briefen aus zwei Jahrhunderten* (Olten and Freiburg: Walter-Verlag, 1977), pp. 42, 67, 100, 115.
9. Charles Wentworth Dilke, *Greater Britain: A Record of Travel in English-speaking Countries during 1866–67* (Philadelphia: J.B. Lippincott, 1869), p. 219.
10. James M. McPherson, *Battle Cry of Freedom: The Civil War Era* (New York: Oxford University Press, 1988), p. 549.
11. Cartoon reprinted in Thomas A. Bailey, *A Diplomatic History of the American People* (Englewood Cliffs, N.J.: Prentice-Hall, 1974), p. 467.
12. Marx to Engels, October 8, 1858, in *On Colonialism: Articles from the New York Tribune and other Writings by Karl Marx and Frederick Engels* (New York: International Publishers, 1972), p. 322.
13. Cited in David Dimbleby and David Reynolds, *An Ocean Apart: The Relationship between Britain and America in the Twentieth Century* (New York: Random House, 1988), p. 25.
14. A. J. P. Taylor, The *Struggle for the Mastery of Europe 1848–1918* (Oxford, Eng.: Clarendon Press, 1954), pp. xxlx–xxx, for detailed figures.
15. Cited by Dimbleby and Reynolds, *An Ocean Apart*, pp. 44.
16. Quoted by Frank Costiglolia, *Awkward Dominion: American Political, Economic, and Cultural Relations with Europe, 1919–1933* (Ithaca, N.Y.: Cornell University Press, 1984), p. 178.

17. Dimbleby and Reynolds, *An Ocean Apart*, pp. 335–36.
18. David Ellwood, "The American Challenge and the Origins of the Politics of Growth," in M. L. Smith and Peter M. R. Stirk, eds., *Making the New Europe: European Unity and the Second World War* (London: Pinter, 1990), pp. 184–200. See also Duignan and Gann, *The Rebirth of the West*, chaps. 1 and 2.
19. Richard Grenier, "Around the World in American Ways," *Public Opinion*, March 1986, pp. 3–5.
20. Paul Hollander, *Anti-Americanism: Critiques at Home and Abroad:1965–1990* (New York: Oxford University Press, 1991). Stephen Haseler, *Anti-Americanism: Steps in a Dangerous Path* (London: Institute for European Defense and Strategic Studies, 1986).
21. Steve Dryden, "Europe in America," *Europe*, June 1991, pp. 6–8. Peter S. Rashid, "Made in Europe," *Europe*, June 1991, pp. 11–12.
22. Haseler, *Anti-Americanism*, pp. 17–18.
23. Ibid., pp. 24–25.
24. Sidney Blumenthal, "Short-Termers: Bush and the CEO's," *New Republic*, 27 January 1992, pp. 15–16.
25. Paul Fussell, *BAD: Or the Dumbing of America* (New York: Summit Books, 1991).
26. "Europe's Open Future," *The Economist*, 22 February 1992, p. 47. "European Immigration," *Christian Science Monitor*, August 1991, p. 22.
27. Richard Bernstein, *Fragile Glory: A Portrait of France and the French* (New York: Alfred A. Knopf, 1990), p. 144.
28. For survey, see Charles Murray, *Losing Ground* (New York: Basic Books), 1984.